CAPITAL, CULTURE, AND THE COMMONS

AKEEL BILGRAMI

Capital, Culture, and the Commons

permanent black in association with ashoka UNIVERSITY

Published by

PERMANENT BLACK

'Himalayana', Mall Road, Ranikhet Cantt,
Ranikhet 263645

perblack@gmail.com

in association with

ASHOKA UNIVERSITY

Distributed by

ORIENT BLACKSWAN PRIVATE LTD

Bangalore Bhopal Bhubaneshwar Chandigarh Chennai
Ernakulam Guwahati Hyderabad Jaipur Kolkata
Lucknow Mumbai New Delhi Patna
www.orientblackswan.com

ISBN 978-81-7824-661-1

For sale in South Asia only

Typeset in Adobe Garamond Pro
by Guru Typograph Technology, Crossings Republic, Ghaziabad
Printed and bound by Manipal Technologies Limited, Manipal

FSC www.fsc.org MIX Paper | Supporting responsible forestry FSC™ C043100 *for*

Zarina

Contents

Fig. 1: David Frazer, *Complicated Life* (2019)

1

Philosophical "Background"

IN HIS REMARKABLE early work, *Birth of Tragedy*, Nietzsche makes much of a distinction that he names, with a typically evocative classical reference, "Apollonian" and "Dionysian",[1] and he allows it to roam over a wide range of seemingly contrasting phenomena: reason and emotion, harmony and chaos, unity and diversity . . . But the contrast, which he reads into the distinction, that I want to focus on in this essay is the one between the representational and the non-representational. It was Nietzsche's driving brief in that work to restore the importance of the latter against what he took to be the gradual ascendancy of the former over several centuries of Western thought and literary production.

In the last century, the contrast between the representational and the non-representational has become familiar to us mostly as a result of the appeal to abstraction in art with a view to repudiating art's aspiration to represent reality – though, as the great historian of art Meyer Schapiro demonstrated, such a repudiation began much earlier, when aesthetic sensibility, tired of the saturation of painting by religious *meaning*, began to turn to *form* as a self-conscious category of aesthetic interpretation and

[1] Friedrich Nietzsche, *The Birth of Tragedy* (1872; rpntd London: Penguin Classics, 1994). Before Nietzsche, Friedrich Hölderlin had also deployed the distinction between the Apollonian and Dionysian, though along somewhat different lines.

assessment. But Nietzsche's turning our attention to the non-representational was not merely to turn us from meaning to form but, more broadly, to turn us from a whole family of discursive phenomena (meaning, truth, knowledge, cognition . . .) to *lived experience* in its non-discursive aspects and practices: sensation, suffering, pleasure, pain, history, memory, culture . . . all expressed – rather than represented – by self and world conceived as Dionysian.

Given Nietzsche's immediate interest in a *literary* form, "tragedy" (not that he allows himself to be much restricted by that interest), some of his concerns are with the representational and non-representational elements within the dramatic arts. His scholarly claim is that in drama, ever since Euripides – he exempts earlier Attic tragedy from this imbalance – there was an increasing emphasis on the Apollonian or representational elements (exemplified in the individual actors on the stage-front and the narrative that they propel in their words and deeds), over the non-discursive Dionysian elements (exemplified in the specific background role provided by the chorus) which came to have a diminishing importance.

When he lifts the restricted focus on the arts and moves on to *philosophy*, Plato's Socrates replaces Euripides as the identified source of this fault line, and "logos" (that particularly language-centred conception of reason) begins to dominate, while a range of linguistically unarticulated experiences are made secondary.

It is interesting that Nietzsche identifies the fault line as early as this. For him, the pre-Socratics had the right balance of Apollonian and Dionysian, and it has been downhill since then. Much of European philosophy since Nietzsche (Heidegger, Derrida) has followed him in this genealogy, describing this longstanding tendency in Western thought as "logocentric". In a different tradition of philosophical scholarship, the fault line is placed at a later date and the particular nature of the "fault" is perhaps more explicitly visible in the way that it spells it out. Thus, for instance, Myles Burnyeat observes that in the Western epistemological tradition, scepticism regarding the external world made a very particular turn in the *Early Modern* period with Descartes.[2] No previous sceptic in the tradition (say, for example, Pyrrhonian skepticism in the Ancient period) had concluded, as Descartes did, that there may not be an external world, from the possibility that we may not have knowledge of the external world. This Cartesian conclusion disallows that there may be other ways of relating to the world than via *knowledge* of it – as perhaps, just *living* in it. It is only with Early Modernity that the very idea of living in the world came to be seen as so mediated by knowledge of it, that to lose knowledge of the world would be to lose the world itself. This diagnosis gives a very precise elaboration of the logocentrism identified in the Nietzschean genealogy, but it places

[2] "Can the Sceptic Live His Scepticism?", in *The Skeptical Tradition*, ed. Myles Burnyeat (Berkeley: University of California Press, 1983).

it at a later date, we may assume, because the saturation of "living" by "knowledge" is assumed to have come about only as a result of the central place that science (then called "natural philosophy") came to have in intellectual culture in the modern period. Aristotelian science did not have the same dominant status in the culture of Europe as modern science came to have, even if there were philosophical premonitions of the logocentrism going as far back as Socrates and Plato.

As I read him, Nietzsche's deepest insight here is more radical than a dismay about a long emerging imbalance between the discursive and non-discursive. Rather, he views the demotion of the Dionysian, as logos came to dominate, as, in the end, a kind of philosophical incoherence, a denial of the *conditions of the possibility of* logos. If I am right in this reading, what is being said is that it is the non-discursive or non-representational, communal (thus, the stress on the chorus) practices and collective memories and experiences that lie behind and make possible the discursively and linguistically articulated, the representational, the knowledgeable forms, that have come to occupy centre stage. Thus, the effort to erase them is not just a distorting imbalance, it is a failure to comprehend their fundamental ineliminability; it is to treat a necessity as a mere (dispensable) contingency. If x makes y conceptually possible, it cannot make coherent sense to allow y to usher x out from centrality and significance.

This suggests that the distinction between the Apollonian and the Dionysian lends itself to another distinction, which came to be emphasised in a range of other philosophers since Nietzsche, the distinction between "foreground" and "background" intended to mark what is *explicit*, the topic of conspicuous focus and discussion, and what is only *implicit* but making possible the contents, indeed the very idea, of whatever it is that is being explicitly discussed.[3] It's just that because it is only in the background and only implicit, the centrality of its enabling role can be missed and even denied. With this further distinction in place, Nietzsche's insight, which I mentioned above, can now be fully articulated as follows: it is only against a *background* of non-discursive human customs and habits and social history and memory that a *foreground* discursive field of explicitly articulated concepts and knowledges make sense and can be what we take them to be.

Not all subsequent philosophy that made this further distinction stresses what Nietzsche, on my reading, is keen to stress, that the idea of the background is predominantly a realm populated by the non-representational and non-discursive.

[3] Heidegger, for instance, but, more recently philosophers such as Herbert Dreyfus, John Searle, and Charles Taylor have also made much use of the notion of a background. Peirce and Wittgenstein do so as well and I discuss them both a little later in the text. I have learnt from all these philosophers, though the use I put the notion to is distinct from how it surfaces in their work.

Charles Sanders Peirce, for example, made insightful use of the idea of a background in his epistemology, but for him the background was fully discursive and representational. In his brilliant essay "The Fixation of Belief",[4] Peirce equates epistemology with the "*enterprise of knowledge*", i.e., with *inquiry* into the truth as undertaken by human subjects; and he presents inquiry as proceeding with two notions, those of "belief", on the one hand, and "hypothesis" or "conjecture", on the other. *From the point of view of the inquirer*,[5] her beliefs simply are true. But she holds various other propositions much more tentatively, as hypotheses. These latter are in the foreground and are the subject of inquiry. Her beliefs are in the background and, qua truths, their role is to implicitly provide the standards by the lights of which inquiry will proceed to decide whether the conjectures in the foreground are to be confirmed or infirmed. If infirmed, a hypothesis will be discarded altogether. If confirmed, a hypothesis will be removed from the foreground and included in the background of beliefs that provide the standards for all subsequent inquiry that seeks to confirm or infirm future hypotheses. Such a notion of "background" as vital to inquiry repudiates

[4] Charles Sanders Peirce, "The Fixation of Belief", *Popular Science Monthly*, 1877, vol. 12, pp. 1–15.

[5] Even if not from someone else's point of view – though this qualification should not need to be made if the inquirer is collectively conceived as a "we".

Cartesian epistemology, which inquires into all propositions at once without any such distinction, seeking to find among them those that are indubitably true – but it does not view the standards by which their truth is to be assessed as being given by a background of implicitly held beliefs that are true; rather the standard for assessment is supposed to be some more intuitive idea of what is "clear and distinct" and "self-evident". Cartesian scepticism that is the outcome of this epistemology, cannot even get started in a Peircean framework. It assumes that we can step outside all of our beliefs and assess them whereas, in Peirce, any given assessment is made by the lights provided by an implicit background of beliefs that are true and – at least while this assessment is taking place – *they* are not up for assessment.

However, for Peirce, the notion of the background is marked only by its implicitness (in contrast with the explicitly formulated hypotheses in the foreground being considered in inquiry), not by non-discursiveness. What is implicitly held in the background are beliefs, with full-blown propositional content, presumed to be true. These are fully discursive, representational phenomena. By contrast, Nietzsche's concerns (as also mine in this essay) assume a notion of the background as a field which, though it may contain some discursive elements like beliefs, is mostly a non-discursive field of practices and customs and habits and social memories. I will proceed, therefore, with the conviction that there is much coincidence (that is to say, coinciding) of the two distinctions I have made: discursive and non-discursive, foreground and background. The discursive coincides with the foreground, and the background is largely non-discursive. This is, no doubt, because my concerns in this essay, as Nietzsche's, are not, as they are in Peirce, merely epistemological in the narrow sense of inquiry into truth.

What, then, are my concerns? Their reach is very broad indeed, taking in political economy, culture, law, and the nature of our political ideals. But let me lead into these concerns by exploring first the idea of "the commons".

2

Capital and the Commons

THE COMMONS is a subject almost impossible to hold in mind without remarking on its diminishment and destruction. We cannot but think of the commons without observing how much they have receded, from the Early Modern period down to the present day, as a result of one or other form of "enclosure" upon them.

Initially, the concept applied mostly to land. Expanses of land that were shared without rivalry, and used by their inhabitants for cultivation or grazing or just simply foraging, were first described as "the commons". Today, the term is used much more widely. Indeed, we sometimes find the term applied to the entire planet Earth. Thus, geologists, for instance, when they first put in to the stratigraphic authorities for a change of name for our current era (from "the Holocene" to "the Anthropocene"), discarded their narrow focus on the lithosphere and declared the Earth's atmosphere, hydrosphere, and biosphere, to be the planetary commons. And, now that that knowledge has burst out of the bounds of books and journals, and out of the confines of academies and libraries, there is constant talk of the knowledge commons and the digital commons. I will focus on the land commons and will relate it to the environmental and other commons as my dialectic unfolds.

The loss of the land commons, as is well known, is genealogically tied to the rise of capital.

In *Das Capital*,[1] Marx discusses at length the "Enclosures Movement" in England and describes, in terms of what he calls "primitive accumulation", the process by which land that was shared without rivalry came to be privatised, generating what has come to be called "agrarian capitalism". Scholars have described the large extent of the commons prior to their privatisation, not just in England but in the European continent as well. Even when a landholder owned a rural estate, the peasantry had a range of what were described as "usufructory" privileges and rights – for growing crops, for grazing stock, for access to water and wood, etc. In flatlands, the "*open* field system", which was a *common* property system, was a widely prevalent form of cultivation of arable ground. All of this changed with the "enclosures", the fencing and subdividing into private plots with full and absolute private rights given to the owners.

Marx himself was highly critical of the brutal and coercive nature of the enclosures and, in being so, he was merely repeating the protest of a vocal and active dissenting tradition in England that goes back to the Lollard Revolt in the fifteenth century and which then flowered with "revolutionary" force in a variety of movements of the radical puritan sects of some two centuries later. It was not till the second half of the seventeenth century

[1] Karl Marx, "Chapter 27", *Das Capital*, vol. 1, pt VIII (1867; rpntd London: Penguin Classics, 1992).

that one found, in Locke's *Second Treatise on Civil Government*,[2] an explicit and fully worked out theoretical rationalisation of the enclosures.[3] By "rationalisation" I mean an account that literally rendered it "rational", presenting an argument that made it seem a political and moral *achievement*.

A loosely reconstructed version of that account, drawing on the famous chapter on property in that work and combining it with various other strands in Locke, including the familiar idea of a social contract, might go as follows. In a conjectural past, there was an originary condition – call it a "state of nature". Its inhabitants one day convene and agree by mutual consent on a certain set of arrangements and principles to live by, thereby immediately transforming the state of nature into a polity and transforming themselves, hitherto merely people, into citizens. This "social contract" is rational, it is said, if no inhabitant is made worse off by these arrangements and many are indeed better off – that is, if there is a Pareto improvement[4] over the state of nature, and

[2] John Locke, *Two Treatises on Government* (1689; rpntd Cambridge: Cambridge University Press, 1988).

[3] There was less explicit, less worked out, advocacy on the part of earlier thinkers such as Bacon, Hartlib, and the circle of "agricultural improvers" whom they influenced.

[4] A "Pareto improvement" is defined by economists to be a change, as, say, in the allocation of resources, such that it makes no one worse off and makes at least one person better off.

if the arrangements and principles to live by are freely consented to by all inhabitants. A standard Lockean construction[5] by which this gets exemplified is this: some among the inhabitants freely

[5] I have used the term "Lockean" deliberately to convey that Locke scholarship has offered other readings than this standard reading I am presenting of the fencing off of land. The reading presented here might claim textual support by pointing out that Locke speaks of labour *very generally* at the initial point where it is supposed to "mix" with soil (as he puts it, all labour at this stage does is "added something . . . more than Nature, the common Mother of all, had done") to justify the privatisation of land property. As a result, one can, at this initial stage, view even the construction of a fence on the soil by an individual to be labour (after all, it is something "added" to the soil that is "more than nature".) It is only later uses of the term "labour" in the text, after money has been authorised and one can buy another's labour and sell one's own labour, that the term comes to have its more usual specific meaning. All I am seeking to put in place here is a familiar sort of construction in the genealogy of capital found in the Early Modern period. Locke, on one standard reading that I present, is a convenient peg to hang the construction on, though a fuller account of it would, no doubt, invoke as well other earlier figures such as Bacon and Hartlib, often described as "improvers" and "reformers". It is Locke alone, though, who situates his argument for privatisation in the contractualist ideal in the way that I present below. I should also add that nothing in Locke's remarks seeking to ensure that the privatisation of land property need not lead to rapaciousness and the exclusion of others from benefiting from it (". . . as much as any one can make use of to any advantage of life before it spoils; so much he may by his labour fix a property in; whatever is beyond this, is more than his share, and belongs to others . . .") undermines his account's place in the genealogy of the loss of the commons that I am presenting.

decide that if any one of them comes upon a portion of the expanse and fences it, and registers the enclosed land with a primitive form of bureau set up for this purpose, he[6] may declare it to be "mine". Others in the group are left out of this process,[7] but they are included in another role: the new possessors of enclosed parts of the land offer them work on their land for wages, something to which these non-possessors of land freely consent. And so, it is claimed that everyone (both the possessors and the non-possessors of property) is better off than they were in the state of nature.

As I said, this argument was widely seen as giving theoretical legitimacy to the privatisation of the commons that the enclosures wrought. But we also know that well before Locke's theoretical accounts, there was widespread resistance to the enclosures in Early Modern England. So, let me introduce a counterargument against this Lockean social contract and put it (anachronistically) in the mouths of some of the dissenters against enclosures in that period, groups such as the Diggers and radical Levellers.[8] (I say "anachronistically" not only because these dissenters predated Locke but also because I will be using

[6] My use of the male version of the personal pronoun here merely keeps faith with the historical reality of Locke's time.

[7] Others are left out, quite obviously, if the land is scarce relative to the population and, in fact, Locke especially mentions America as a kind of outsize place of plenitude.

[8] I say "radical" Levellers deliberately. As emerged very clearly in the Putney Debates, many Levellers advocated the privatisation of the commons.

a vocabulary in the formulation of the counterargument that is ours, not theirs.) Let us, then, ventriloquise onto the lips of the most prominent of the dissenters, Gerard Winstanley, the following counterargument appealing to the notion of what economists call an "opportunity cost". (An opportunity cost is an *avoided* benefit when we make a certain decision.) He says to Locke: "You are right, the privatisation of the land and the recruitment of wage labour to work on the land does make everyone better off than they were in the state of nature, but it does not make them better off than they *would have been* if the land was not privatised in the first place and there was a collective cultivation of the commons instead."

The response to Locke that I have attributed to Winstanley explicitly mentions the commons, taking what Locke called a "state of nature" to be the commons, and claiming that we have a choice that Locke's argument overlooks: we could think of it as Locke does, but there is an opportunity cost in doing so. It avoids the alternative of thinking of it in terms of its collective cultivation.

The matter cannot be said to rest here because a subsequent well-known move in the conceptual genealogy of the privatised ideal can be read as precisely arguing, on behalf of Locke, that a central assumption made by this counterargument from opportunity cost, is untenable. This is the assumption that there is a cogent ideal of the collective cultivation of the commons. It has been famously argued that the assumption is not cogent at all.

Here, in the broadest stroke, is how that familiar argument goes, appealing to the game-theoretic framework of a multi-person prisoners' dilemma.[9] The intractable problem is supposed to be that, given human psychology, individual commoners are rationally required to behave in ways that undermine the collective; they are required to not co-operate in the ways necessary to sustain the collective. The co-operation necessary for the collective ideal requires that each commoner pay a certain cost (sometimes – in fact oftentimes – this cost takes the form of restraint, since overuse or overcultivation is often the problem). If each individual commoner pays the cost, of course everyone gains. But each individual commoner will have to consider that if he does not co-operate (i.e. does not pay the cost), the gains are immediate, whereas the gains from co-operation are long-term; moreover, the gains from non-cooperation are all for himself, whereas the gains from paying the cost are spread over the whole group. Above all – and this is really the crucial and clinching consideration to which I will keep returning – he is never sure that if he pays the cost others will do so, too. Since one is in the epistemic dark about whether others are contributing the bit demanded of

[9] This argument, whose conclusion is that the very idea of a commons which can be collectively cultivated, is doomed to failure and "tragedy" represents a widespread outlook of modern, "liberal" political economy, and can be found implicitly in many theoretical accounts. For a well-known explicit statement of a version of the argument, see Garrett Hardin's well-known essay, "The Tragedy of the Commons", *Science*, 1968, vol. 162, no. 3859, pp. 1243–8.

them in the collective cultivation, one constantly fears that one's contribution will be wasted if others don't do their bit.[10] On such an understanding of the collective ideal, an individual commoner who decides not to co-operate is always at an advantage since the gains of non-cooperation will be immediate, and all for himself and completely assured, whereas the gains from co-operating are long-term, dispersed over the whole group and, above all, *always uncertain*. Non-cooperation for him, as an individual, would thus be rational. But the commons cannot survive if each individual does this individually rational thing. It is doomed. Thus, "the tragedy of the commons". So, privatisation is a better bet.

To this familiar game-theoretic updating of Locke, there has tended to be a standard response. The spectre of the tragedy of the commons is exaggerated; the commons is not doomed to tragedy since it can be governed by regulation, that is to say by policing and punishing non-cooperation.

Now, who can be against such regulation? It is obviously a good thing. What is less obvious is whether the idea of regulation itself escapes the kind of thinking that goes into generating the tragedy of the commons. The thinking just occurs (or recurs)

[10] I am stressing this epistemic anxiety more than other considerations that drive the so-called "dominance argument" because it is what I want to fasten on to bring out what I eventually have to say about the mentality of alienation.

one step up. Even if we ignore the well-known difficulties of detecting many non-obvious forms of non-cooperation, the question arises: why should someone co-operate with policing and detection and punishment if they can get away with *not* co-operating – by offering bribes, for instance, or making mafia-style threats against those who detect and police or those who co-operate with the policing and detecting (witnesses, for example)? And in societies that pride themselves on having overcome a culture of bribes and threats, non-cooperation can be (and is) pursued by loopholing the laws and regulations to make non-cooperation legal after all. Thus, though we should obviously support regulation, to view the possibility of regulation as a reason for not probing more deeply is to merely illustrate the treadmill cast of mind that finds itself constantly dogged by the thinking that generates the "tragedy" of the commons, and that *mentality* cannot be rectified by solutions like regulation. What is worth exploring, then, is something that allows us to dismount the treadmill, something that only an alternative way of thinking can offer. Einstein once said that we cannot solve our problems within the thinking that we used when we created them. How, then, might one probe the possibility that the mentality itself is not compulsory?[11]

[11] Elinor Ostrom's fine analytical and extensive empirical study, *Governing the Commons: The Evolution of Institutions for Collective Action* (1990; rpntd Cambridge: Cambridge University Press, 1998), for instance,

To repeat, the question of regulation via law and norm and their application in policing and punishment requires co-operation just as much as the collective cultivation of the commons does, and the mentality (elevated into a form of rationality) that drives the tragedy of the commons argument should therefore be operative one step up and threaten to undermine regulation by law as well. How do we get past this mentality and this impasse? The Lockean tradition would have it that there is no getting past it, but arguably this triumphant assumption on its part is only something it came to because it was looking at the wrong place for an answer. So, questions arise: where does it look for answers, why does it not find them there, and where else might one look?

---

presents the principles for such regulation after a scrutiny of various commons and their governance in four continents. The work is particularly interesting because it seeks to expound non-centralised forms of governance in which some of the alternative ways of thinking I am gesturing at might even potentially be exemplified, thus *combining* regulation with the deeper goal. See also her 2009 Nobel Prize acceptance speech, "Beyond Markets and States: Polycentric Governance of Complex Economic Systems". These are all issues well worth exploring in detail, and the present book makes a philosophical start at such an exploration.

Fig. 2: David Frazer, *The Deal* (2015)

3

The Cultural Commons as Background

I HAVE BEEN saying that the subject of the commons is really the subject of its loss. And I have given a broad sketch of the *conceptual* genealogy of that loss in theoretical arguments that legitimise the enclosure and privatisation of the commons, while also setting up a dialectic in which those arguments are disputed and defended. All this raises a large question about how we might seek to address the questions of the loss of the commons that is so often made to seem like an inevitable development in the unfolding of our modernity.

So far, however, I have only presented the story of its loss, I have not really said very much by way of trying to define or characterise what the commons exactly are. The only defining feature I have mentioned is that the commons are *shared* by their inhabitants without rivalry. A second defining feature, which has been more true of the land and environmental commons, but is increasingly true of the knowledge commons as well, is that their inhabitants *sustain* themselves on them. We might say that these are the two minimal features that any notion of the commons must satisfy.

However, these defining characteristics of "sharing" and "being sustained by" are bound to appear in very different forms, depending on whether the inhabitants of any particular commons conceive of *themselves as a group* or not. If the inhabitants simply forage or cultivate relatively independent of each other, as individuals or, at best, individual families, say, then "sharing" and "being sustained by" are relatively simple notions. But if these individuals begin to view themselves as a group, then "sharing" presumably takes on quite a complex hue, bringing in such things as shared understandings and unselfconscious relations of trust that make for side-by-side communal life as a group. (I say "unselfconscious" quite deliberately because, as I keep stressing, the background is marked by non-explicit and non-discursively constituted relations.) So also, being "sustained by" now means more than just surviving biologically as individuals, but sustaining as well whatever it is that makes and binds the group as a group in its own self-conception: kinship, as it might be, or religion, or caste, or even "citizenship" . . . Thus the very idea of the commons becomes a much more complex notion once the inhabitants of the commons view themselves as a group, something that presumably happened very early on indeed in the land commons. It is these complexities that we need to explore if we are going to address the large questions that we raised at the tail end of the last chapter.

Let me explore them first by stepping into the footprint of a routine idea we have inherited from a largely conjectural cultural anthropology. The earliest forms of group self-conception took the form of kinship relations; and though it is not necessary to view kinship relations as consisting of *blood* ties (there are other notions of kinship), to keep things simple let us assume that initially these were the ties that bound the group. (Nothing in my argument will depend on this assumption, the argument can be adapted to other ways of understanding kinship.) A question that immediately arises is how did groups that conceived of themselves as a group along kinship lines bound by blood ties move on to other forms of self-conception that were less naturalistic and more, as the jargon goes, "constructed". What agencies brought about such a transformation?

It is just here that the notion of a "background" with which I opened this essay in the first section, impresses with its relevance.

If there were analogues in the cultural sphere to evolutionary accounts, we might suggest that this transformation away from naturalistic kinship ties to more constructed ties occurred due to a cultural "mutation". But one has to assume that any idea of such a mutation when it comes to culture is just a placeholder for more detailed accounts of a conjectural social history. (By "conjectural", I just mean to gesture towards a familiar method in social and political philosophy exemplified, for instance, by the notion of a "social contract", whereby one *posits* an historical event – since no one actually has any historical evidence of anyone convening to draw up or endorse any such contract – with a view to developing explanatory claims about society and politics.) One such account might go like this.

In kinship relations, conflicts are bound to arise about one thing or another. To resolve them, no appeal to considerations within kinship ties will suffice since *both* parties to the conflict would be related by those ties. So, in order to resolve the conflict, one would have to step back and construct, from within one's practices and habits and often implicit and unspoken conventions, some criteria – for adjudication of the conflict – that transcends those ties. That is, from within a background of those ongoing practices and customs, one would have to articulate anew some notion that doesn't mention kinship relations and speaks more generally. One might, thus, find oneself saying while assessing some aspect of the conflict, "we should treat like cases alike and we should see x as a *relevant* similarity but y as an *irrelevant* one", where what substitutes for the variables, though not understood along kinship lines, may not yield anything yet that would amount to criteria we would describe in terms of "fairness", "justice", etcetera (though, of course, it is possible that a path may be generated in that eventual direction). But, however parochial still, it is only by the applications of such notions that one could resolve the intra-kin conflicts that have arisen. These notions may now become explicitly articulated *foregrounded* principles for conflict resolution, even though they were drawn from a background of an unspoken, mostly non-discursive repertory of customs and habits and practices, as I said. And eventually a *tradition* would emerge in which these foregrounded principles might recede to unspoken and implicit background practices and new foregrounded principles would emerge from the tradition, by a similar process.

I say all this to emphasise that when we consider individuals, sharing and sustaining themselves on the commons, coming to have, via this kind of process, a socially constructed (rather than kinship-based) group self-conception, we are presented with a fundamental and unavoidable distinction. This is just a specific application of the distinction that I read into Nietzsche in my opening pages. So applied, it distinguishes between, on the one hand, a field of conflict and resolution of conflict by explicit criteria or principles of adjudication that may be said to be in the "foreground" and, on the other, a wide range of unselfconscious habits, practices, customs, and ways of being that are implicit and often non-discursive and in the "background", yet are vital to enabling (or, as philosophers like to say, are "the conditions for the possibility" of) what goes on much more conspicuously in the foreground. In a word, it is a distinction between the realm of codification in the form of law or explicit norm, and the more discretionary realm of unselfconscious custom and habit that lies below its surface and makes possible both its articulation and its implementation. And I want to suggest that of this background phenomenon, so understood, one can make five quite striking propositions.

First, they may quite properly be thought of as the *cultural commons*. Second, they are, by their very nature, a necessarily *non-cancellable and non-optional commons*, even when many of the other commons have, in one way or other, suffered increasing cancellation and increasingly appear to be optional as a result of a variety of forms of "enclosure" visited upon them. Third, it is in the cultural commons, in this sense, that we may find the conceptual sources for the recovery or partial recovery of the commons that are increasingly subjected to cancellation and relegated to optionality. Fourth, the cultural commons, as I understand it, have the unusual property of amounting to or exemplifying an ideal, but one that, unlike many other ideals, does *not appear to be an ideal when it is working*. And, finally, it would be no stretch or distortion to say that, qua ideal, what I have called the cultural commons exemplifies a more general version of the specific ideal that Marx had in mind when he specified the way in which workers *fall short of it* in the alienation they suffer in being estranged from each other[1] – or, to put it more plainly, the ideal of an unalienated life and society.

I have made two claims in this book so far that I will want to now make the basis of spelling out these propositions regarding the cultural commons.

1. The cultural commons reside in a background that lies implicitly behind and makes possible a foreground field of explicit law and norm.

[1] Such estrangement *from each other* (as opposed to from their work, the product of their work, etc.) is the last of the four senses of alienation that Marx elaborated in *Economic and Philosophical Manuscripts of 1844*. I say "more general" version because, given my more broadly philosophical interests here, I am not focused on labour in particular, as Marx's rich and detailed specification of alienation was.

2. When inhabitants of the commons begin to conceive of themselves as a group, the notions that define the commons ("sharing" and 'sustaining") undergo a complexification, with sharing now involving shared understandings and unselfconscious relations of trust among the members of the group (even if not with others outside the group), and sustaining now demanding not just physical survival of individual inhabitants of the commons but also the keeping going of whatever it is that makes the group a group – the idea here is that this precisely means keeping going the shared understandings and relations of trust that "sharing" itself has come to mean. That looped interrelation between sharing and sustaining is an essential part of the complexity that is introduced into the defining features of the commons.

In the next chapter, I will successively draw out the implications of (1) and (2), arguing that (1) makes possible the very concept and content of explicit laws and norms, and (2) makes possible *their implementation.* In the drawing out of these twin implications, the hope is that the five propositions regarding the cultural commons will have unfolded.

Fig. 3: David Frazer, *200 Words* (2021)

4

The Cultural Commons and the Very Concept (and Content) of Law

THE IDEA IN (1) is that norms and laws explicitly formulated in the foreground by a social group necessarily presuppose a background of habit, shared expectation, customs, and unspoken assumptions, as well as social memory, all of which constitute a set of cultural practices that over time become a tradition from within which members of the group conceive of themselves as a group. This background is what I have been saying deserves the name "cultural commons". I will first present the idea at a level more abstract than the legal and the political and then see it through to these more specific domains.

Consider, for instance, an example discussed by Ludwig Wittgenstein in his well-known discussion of "following a rule" or norm.[1] Wittgenstein's eventual interest is in rules of language use, but the example he illustrates his ideas with is one of a road sign, an arrow pointing in a certain direction.

Whence the directive and regulative power of this sign that expresses a rule or norm to tell us to "turn left", say? How do the members of a group within which the sign has this directive power of a norm come to see it that way? It certainly can't be a matter of just free interpretation on the part of those who see the sign. It is not as if the sign is seen merely as a physical configuration on

[1] Ludwig Wittgenstein, *Philosophical Investigations* (1953; rpntd Oxford: Wiley-Blackwell, 2009).

a board to which each person who sees it gives a meaning or significance by an act of interpretation. Rather, each person in the group immediately and literally sees the sign as directing him or her to turn left. That is, the sign is seen as *meaningful* right from the outset (in the *seeing* itself); it is not first seen as a purely physical configuration to which meaning has to be added by an interpretative feat that the viewer has to perform. Thus, we literally *see meaning* or normative significance or directive ruling *in* the sign when we see it. But what makes for this rich phenomenology of seeing meaning or norm and not merely a physical mark on a wooden board? What underlies this perceptual sensitivity in the group to signs of this kind – a sensitivity that a visitor from an alien group might not possess and for whom no such directiveness may be apparent in the perception, with the lines on the wooden post being just that, lines on wood and no more, and who would then have to struggle to find an interpretation?

Wittgenstein's expression "forms of life" (which is frequently to be found in his later work) is intended to capture the range of *background practices* in the group's tradition that I mentioned which literally gives sight to the group when it comes to reading such a road sign. We can make up a story in the background for this particular example. Let us say that members of the group have a social memory, accumulated through a long tradition of oral relay, books, comics, films, and so on, of a set of practices in which arrows were or are used with bows to shoot at various targets and so have come to associate the direction of the flight of the arrow with its head in front as the direction with which the sign is associated. (In fact, that it should be thought of as the head is, of course, itself determined by the background "forms of life".) We can also imagine that in another culture where arrows were merely used for decorative purposes and not for shooting, no such directional association of an arrow's flight takes hold in the mentality of its members and instead (with sufficient details added) what gets associated with the arrow's head is the place of origin rather than the sought destination. These details apart, the point is that it is only such a background of cultural practices (say, target shooting and martial weaponry versus decorative purposes) within which the sign's normative or rule directiveness of one or another kind is so much as possible in the foreground. The physical sign, qua physical, tells us nothing. It is only acculturation in a tradition of practices that makes possible to members of the group the sign's meaning and normative directiveness. There is no understanding the foregrounded field, therefore, where rules and norms and laws are in play (traffic rules and laws, in this instance), without a taken-for-granted background of practices and social memory and implicitly shared assumptions.

The implications of this, in general, for the law and for explicit regulations in the realm of state and public policy are plain to see. We would not have any good sense of what laws are and what they mean and say and direct us to, if we did not have a background of far less discursive and far less explicitly articulated tradition of shared practices. We are often reminded of this when things go amiss. There can be spectacular cases of mismatch that bring it out vividly. I believe Joan of Arc provides one such. Here was a mystic poet, warrior-saint, with no acculturation into the practices and unspoken shared assumptions that lay behind the law and its protocols to which she was subjected in a courtroom. It is small wonder that she was convicted. Everything in her background of practices and customs left her ill-prepared and ill-suited for the courtroom, with tragic consequences, not just her conviction but also her complete and abject failure to even so much as comprehend the zeitgeist within which she had to present her defence, making the conviction a foregone conclusion. In fact, those who thought her insane may not have even quite seen that in the face of such wholesale incomprehension of the culture whereby the law is rendered "rational", she had no other option or strategy but to declare herself to be irrational.

Less spectacular, subtler cases of mismatch reveal the same point. It was widely said by sociologists of the welfare state that for the first decade or more of the functioning of the National Health Service in post-war Britain, the class for whom it was primarily set up was the least able to exploit the benefits it offered since these citizens were just not at home (not brought up to be at home) in the culture that underlies the complicated set of rules that characterised the dispensation of the benefits. As a result, it was the educated middle class that was most able to take advantage of the benefits, until gradual acculturation into the background practices underlying the foregrounded rules made these latter more straightforwardly intelligible and easier to navigate.[2] In a word, without upbringing and participation in a *cultural* commons in the background, the law in the foreground remains opaque, much like the road sign remains merely paint on wood rather than a rule or norm.

A different kind of case may be found in the utterly familiar problems that were generated when migrant communities of labour arrived from the erstwhile colonies into European nations in the second half of the twentieth century, bringing with them a "background" (a "cultural commons") very different from, indeed mismatched with, the background (the cultural commons) of the European citizens among whom they had landed. Few governments showed the requisite sensitivity in handling these problems, however. In fact, recently, even so prominent a figure

[2] See Josiah Ober, *Democracy and Knowledge: Innovation and Learning in Classical Athens* (Princeton: Princeton University Press, 2009), for an interesting discussion of how this sort of failure was precisely what Athenian democracy sought to pre-empt by exposing the law to discussion in meetings "in the round" so that all could see and hear each other and see and hear what all others knew.

of the European Left as Slavoj Žižek, who made an impeccably correct diagnosis that the causes of refugee migration from the Middle East to European nations are a result of imperialist interventionist policies (invasions, embargoes, etc.) by European nations and the United States, then declared that European nations should make clear that though the refugees are welcome for this reason, they should also understand well that they must accept our ways of life, our laws and norms, or else be subject to harsh state repression and punishment.[3] With such insensitive attitudes, a total unwillingness to allow a new cultural commons to evolve through mutual engagement between guest and host communities, it is hardly surprising that acute problems have arisen over a wide range of matters in the foreground of the law, including such fundamental issues as free speech and the censorship of perceived blasphemy. These are the hard issues raised by a recognition of the background–foreground distinction that I am insisting on.[4]

[3] Slavoj Žižek, "The Non-Existence of Norway", *London Review of Books*, 10 September 2015, vol. 37, no. 17.

[4] The idea of an engagement between guest and host communities is with a view to leading to a new social contract which the guests come to accept as a result of the engagement rather than just have it be imposed on them, something to which they must willy-nilly acquiesce in simply because they are guests. A vivid, if very trivial, example of an outcome of a new contract in which guests are participants might be found in the fact that today very often you find a host at a dinner asking a guest whether she may smoke *in her own home!*

5

The Cultural Commons and the Implementation of the Law

I TURN, THEN, TO (2). If the very concept and content of regulation and law in the foreground presupposes the idea of a set of background non-discursive customs and practices and social history that form a cultural commons, the law's *implementation* presupposes a particular characteristic of these cultural commons that form once individuals see themselves as a group – something that I had described in my claim regarding unselfconscious relations of trust among members of the group (even if not with those outside the group), relations that sustain them as a group. Once again, before taking up questions of law and politics, let me initially approach the idea at a more abstract level by looking to a basic enabling condition that allows individuals to conceive of themselves as members of a group: the communicative aspects of language.

In a careful analysis of the concept of human communicative meaning, the philosopher H.P. Grice[1] proposes that a complicated set of nested intentions on the part of speakers underlies the nature of human linguistic communication. He first points out that it does not suffice to say that a speaker means something if he or she merely intends to get something across to someone (call him or her the "hearer"). Of course, it is necessary that one has that intention, but that intention alone will not be sufficient. Thus, Iago placing a handkerchief in a suitably revealing

[1] "Meaning", *Philosophical Review*, 1957, vol. 66, no. 3, pp. 377–88.

place with the intention of getting something across to Othello is not what goes on in linguistic communication, which is overt and not, as with Iago, covert and manipulative. So, one needs to add a second intention for communicative meaning: that one intends the hearer to recognise that one is intending to convey something to him or her. And then Grice asks a crucial further question. If someone overtly showed someone a photograph of some scene (x talking to y in the college quadrangle, say) with the intention of conveying to her that x was talking to y in the college quadrangle, would that count as a case of human communication of the sort that goes on in language? No, says Grice, it would not, because even though this is overtly done, the *photograph* – being the sort of thing it is – would convey that information to the hearer *directly and by itself* and the hearer coming to have that information about x and y would not be done via the recognising of the detailed communicative intentions of the speaker.

This is a very subtle and crucial point. What Grice means by the photograph "directly and by itself" conveying the information, bypassing the speaker's intentions, is that – on the assumption that photographs don't lie – upon seeing the photograph, the hearer is immediately informed by the photograph of the information. The speaker hasn't told the hearer the information, the hearer has come to have that information by the photograph itself, and the speaker's intentions are not doing the communicative work in the reception of the hearer. That is, the photograph conveys the information *anyway*, making the speaker's intentions to convey it inessential to the process by which the hearer comes to have the information. Compare this, Grice says, to the speaker drawing or painting for the hearer (or viewer, in this case) a picture of x talking to y in the quadrangle. Now, we have human communication in the full sense that one finds in language. Drawings, unlike photographs, require the hearer (viewer) to acquire the information via a grasp of the full range of intentions that the speaker has; the information is not conveyed anyway by the drawing, as it is by the photograph – that being the difference between drawings and photographs. (Essential to this point that Grice is making is the assumption that photographs don't lie. Someone might object that in this age of spin, as we well know, people can just doctor photographs or even *create* them in a dark room with chemicals and paper so long as there is a shaft of light from the outside, but I think Grice would have argued, surely correctly, that these are not photographs but rather drawings or paintings with photographic materials.[2] Photographs are not defined by their superficial look or appearance, they are defined rather by the fact of having

[2] After all, we make paintings with just about any material (just some months ago I saw a painting by Bontecou made partly of *hay*), so why not with chemicals, glossy paper, etc.? I should add here that to bring out this property of verisimilitude of photographs, I have deliberately chosen certain examples of photographs such as one of a scene in which x is talking to y. This is to avoid complications such as when it is said that someone is or is

a specific sort of *causal link* between the photographs and what they are photographs of. If one has no such causal link and just plays with photographic materials in a dark room or on a computer to produce a representation of x talking to y in the college quadrangle that looks like a photograph, one should count that as a painting, not a photograph.)

To ensure, then, that the hearer goes via the intentions of the speaker to acquire the information that, say, x was speaking to y in the quadrangle, Grice says the speaker must have a third intention: the intention that the hearer acquire the information *as a result of* recognising the intention on the part of the speaker to convey that information. That rules out the photograph, but includes the drawing and all the usual linguistic utterances we make to each other in ordinary communication that is typical of the phenomenon of language in its social aspect.[3]

---

not photogenic, i.e., when photographs are said to capture or not capture what a face really looks like. It is sufficient for my purposes that there are cases of the kind I have chosen to illustrate what Grice has in mind in his talk of photographs by themselves conveying certain information. The idea is not to deny that there are ever cases in which photographs don't capture a very revealing likeness of what they are photographs of, but rather to assert that there are clear cases in which photographs directly present information about events and occurrences and objects that they are photographs of.

[3] Here I am not referring to the notion of language that Chomsky has made his subject in his lifelong work in theoretical linguistics. Chomsky

But now notice a very striking implication of what is registered about the nature of language and communication by the need for this third intention. What it shows is that the *possibility* of misrepresentation and lying is essential for something to count as a case of communication as it is found in language. If there is no such possibility of lying and misrepresentation, we don't have a case of linguistic communication, even if we get things across to people. But, on the other hand, and equally obviously, if linguistic communication is going to be effective at all, misrepresentation and lying *can't be ubiquitous either*. Communication breaks down if lying and misrepresentation are pervasive. So, there are twin requirements on language, which pull in different directions: one is that there must be the possibility of something (misrepresentation and lying), and the other is that the actualisation of this possibility is only exceptional and occasional and not routine. What this discussion invoking Grice's analysis brings out, then, is that the notion of trust and reliability is vital to the communicative efficacy of language, and since linguistic communication is a central enabling condition

---

is working with a notion of language that comes with our genetic endowment and grows into a full-fledged faculty and, as such, the social and communicative aspect of language (indeed even its vocalisation and externalisation) is a contingent and ancillary development. Grice's subject – as also, for obvious reasons, mine, in this book – on the other hand is only and wholly this contingent and ancillary development.

of individuals coming to form a group and conceiving of themselves as a group, it is vital, in turn, to this self-conception.[4] The point is so obvious that it hardly needs saying. You stop someone on the street and ask her the time and she looks at her watch and *tells* you. It is the telling that is communicative. If she showed you the watch, your coming to know the time would be done directly by what you see when you look at the watch, bypassing the overt communicative intentions on her part to convey the time to you by showing you the watch. But if she is telling you and not showing you her watch, you have to trust her to not be lying and misinforming you, and we do this unselfconsciously and by and large without exception. Trust is the default. One has to be aware of some unusual circumstance to put the trust on hold. And for the most part the trust is deserved – most people are not waiting to mislead you by telling you the wrong time when you ask them.

This point about language is manifestly generalisable. If such a background of trust in everyday relations within the group informs the everyday practices and customs and habits that lie behind and make possible the very possibility of the group's language, it also constitutes the cultural commons that make possible the very idea of law (and norm) and its implementation in the foreground.

[4] For a discussion of trust and its place in the concept of meaning as is found in Grice's analysis, see Carol Rovane, *The Bounds of Agency* (Princeton: Princeton University Press, 1997).

Consider a simple case of the regulations or laws of cricket. In a Test match in the infamous "Bodyline" series of 1932–3, a player of one side is quoted as having said: "There are two sides playing out there in the field, but only one of them is playing cricket." Yet the side that he was criticising for not playing cricket did not over the five days of the game commit one single act that violated any of the laws that constituted the game they were playing. Within the strict adherence to those laws, a wide range of actions were being perpetrated that made it clear to vast numbers of observers and commentators and players on the other side that what the laws *were for* – i.e. the game of cricket that the laws constituted – was not attained in that game.

This can happen even when one has the best of intentions and not the dark ones that one of those sides was displaying on the field. Take, for example, a company's well-intentioned resolve to set up what are called "ethical" codes for auditing to make sure that the company is, say, ecologically sound, or fair in its trading practices. It is often reported that in many companies such audits deteriorate into a ritualised ticking off of boxes so that the company can congratulate itself for its virtue, but this amounts to no more than a formal and relatively shallow observance of laws while a wide range of actions that pass the audit remain distinctly harmful to the environment or fail in whatever other protective purpose the laws were formulated for. Another crudely amusing example was recently in the news, when campus rules against utterance of obscenities in public were all strictly followed by students who sat next to each other in groups of four, each wearing a T-shirt with the letter F and U and so forth. No rule could be found against any of them to punish this. Adding another rule *ex post* to the rule book to cover this sort of behaviour could just generate new and more ingenious behaviour of this kind to flout it, and soon the rule book would be a vast and insanely complex almanac that would and could only be understood and kept track of by lawyers, turning the whole field into a cesspool of professionalised expertise, as we already know from even a glance at the small print that accompanies a wide array of medicines and medical procedures. All these examples show that, in the end, nothing short of a background of mutual trust in relations in the members of a group can ensure that the law will not be finessed in myriad unforeseen ways. None of this is to say that the law and regulation are not necessary; it is only to say that their effectiveness in the foreground depends fundamentally and ultimately on the character of the relations of trust that lie in the background and have no discursively explicit articulation and rule book that codifies them.

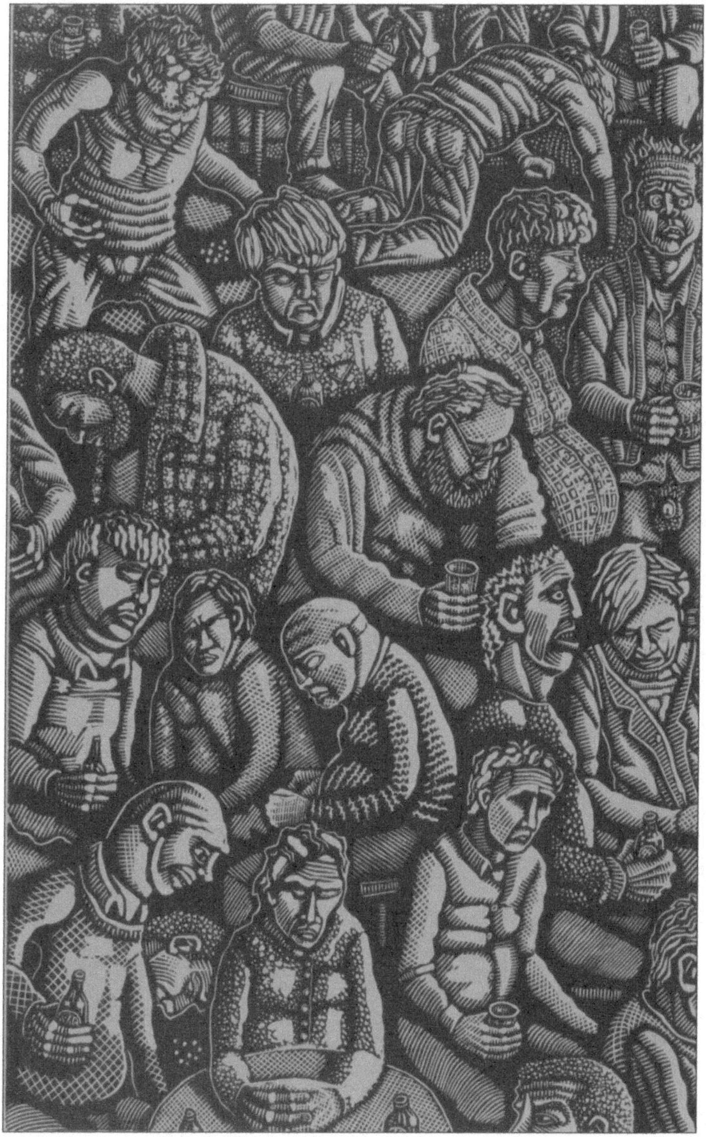

Fig. 4: David Frazer, *Happy Hour II* (2017)

6

First Steps Towards a Response to the Lockean Challenge

We have arrived at something of a punchline, then, on the questions we had left hanging. The long Lockean tradition of thought on this subject comes to its conclusions only because of the way in which it poses its problem. That question was: why is not the solution to the prospect of the tragedy of the commons that appeals to the regulation of the commons via laws formulated and implemented against non-cooperation subject to being undermined by the same considerations that undermined the commons in the first place? To put the question that way is to assume that if the problem arises in the foreground – where law and norm are formulated and regulation on their basis is implemented – its solution must lie in the foreground too. But that assumption is wrong. The resources towards a solution lie in the background, and this background of a cultural commons – without which the foreground's laws could not so much as be formulated meaningfully – is not even recognised by that tradition. Indeed, the very distinction between the foreground and the background is completely unacknowledged by it.

This is a point of some significance in the intellectual history of these subjects. Much of Foucault's anxiety about the emergence of a form of penality with the Enlightenment (not that he puts it in the way I am about to, I am presenting his anxieties in terms of the conceptual distinction I have been making here) was precisely that the foreground of law and regulation was claiming to be all the ground there is.[1] So understood, the anxiety is not (as he puts it) that the discretionary element possessed by magistrates in the penal system of the ancien régime was removed in a new episteme of a more strictly codified understanding of the law, but rather (this is my way of putting it) a background of discretionary, often inarticulate practices and customs and habits that underlie the law's effectiveness in the foreground was refused recognition, and the foreground of the discursive formulations of law and norm was usurping all the ground there was. But, in a quite strict sense, if my entire argument is right, *the very idea of such usurpation is a conceptual incoherence.* There is no understanding, let alone implementing, what is in the foreground if the foreground were all the ground there is.

What cannot be denied, of course, is that all the many examples of the sort I gave above of how laws and norms are often finessed reflect how we can lapse from the relations of trust that regulation by law presupposes in the cultural commons in the background; obviously the point cannot be that such lapses from those relations of trust never occur, but that it is only because those relations exist that the law is implemented to the considerable extent that it is. The cultural commons' relation to the law is thus *constitutive*. In this respect, such a commons amounts to

[1] These anxieties are well known as one of the prominent themes of his *Discipline and Punish* (Paris: Gallimard, 1975).

an ideal in much the same way that principles of rationality are ideals that are constitutive of the very idea of human thought. We can lapse from them, we can be irrational by being inconsistent in some of our beliefs, say, or by displaying intransitivities in our desires, but it would not be thought or thinking we possess, if such irrationality was pervasive.[2]

It may sometimes even be the case that there is quite an extensive lapse or breakdown of these relations of trust in the background. The argument I am making, therefore, should not be seen as encouraging any kind of complacence.[3] In fact, I would read the fascinating and profound transitional moment in South Africa as a case in which Bishop Tutu and his colleagues (including Mandela) – having realised that, as a result of the long and searing experience of apartheid, those relations of trust

[2] For a familiar and rightly admired account of this constitutive role of the ideals of rationality to thought, see Donald Davidson's various essays in his *Inquiries into Truth and Interpretation* (Oxford: Oxford University Press, 1981).

[3] I am keen to stress this because the last time I presented these ideas in a seminar, a common, if elementary, misunderstanding that surfaced in the discussion is that I am, in effect, denying that there is a great deal of inner conflict within a group. There is nothing whatever in what I say that amounts to a denial of this. As I've said more than once in this book, it is the very *existence* of conflicts within a group (and their adjudication) that presupposes a background of a cultural commons with the features that I've described. I would go so far as to say that the conflicts would not even be so much as recognisable as conflicts if there was not such a background with those features, though I won't try to elaborate that here.

in the background had broken down far too extensively in their society – devised something quite dramatically novel for the criminal trial of "transitional" justice with a very specific end in mind. They sought to correct that damage to the trust that is normally present implicitly and unselfconsciously in the background, by modelling transitional criminal law in the foreground explicitly and self-consciously on the model of these relations of trust rather than on the standard procedures of criminal law. They roughly argued:

> We have to live side by side with our past oppressors now, so let us not judge them forensically in a traditional court of law, seeking and presenting evidence in a disengaged mode, while they sit silently in the dock; let us not assess them in that detached mode, applying our norms and laws, let us engage with them, seeking truths about the past through that engagement, trusting them to present the truth of their perpetration of crimes, and look to what correction these confessions make possible for our future together.

But again, if my conceptual analysis is right, even that fascinatingly innovative strategy of a thoroughly revisionary model of law in the foreground will have presupposed its own background of shared assumptions and conventions that amount to a cultural commons. You can sometimes make something that is routinely only implicit and inarticulate explicit in discursive formulations, but only against *its* own background of unspoken assumptions and shared expectations. There is no getting past the idea of a background of cultural commons.

What this reveals is that the term "trust" that I have been using freely and repeatedly in characterising these customs and practices in the background of the cultural commons is not quite the right word for the ideal that the cultural commons exemplifies. It is convenient to use it because it is the most obvious word or concept at hand, and it has been the subject of much sophisticated theorising in recent years. Trust, as the South African experimental moment makes clear, can be foregrounded in an explicit formulation of what is being displayed in a formal trial. In this respect, the concept of trust is like the concept of co-operation. We found, for instance, that responses to the argument for the tragedy of the commons claimed that co-operation can be enforced by policing and punishment of non-cooperation. Policing and punishment with the application of laws is precisely a foreground phenomenon. So, these overused terms ("trust", "co-operation") can characterise tacit and inarticulate features of human relations but they can also be brought to the discursive forefront in explicit formulations. Let me then discard them and explore more carefully the nature of the ideal that the cultural commons, playing the background role I have given it, most deeply expresses.

Quite apart from their susceptibility to being foregrounded in explicitly formal and discursive formulations, the inappropriateness of explicitly normative terms like "trust" and "co-operation" to describe the social relations typical of the cultural commons lies partly in the fact that these terms give the impression that what is being proposed via the very idea of a cultural commons is a sort of moral (or moralistic) critique of a notion of self-interest which, when assumed to be motivating the actions of individuals, causes individuals to put trust and co-operation aside. I think, by contrast, it is important to present the idea of the cultural commons, and the work it is doing in my argument, in a light that stresses not the moralistic aspects of such a critique but, as I said at the end of chapter 2, an alternative mentality that does not even appear as a moral ideal *when it is working*. It is not so much a matter of declaring the idea of self-interest to be morally wrong but rather a matter of what does and does not arise in one's mind or mentality. Thus, to the extent that the ideal exemplified in the cultural commons is working, it is, as it were, an epistemological or cognitive achievement. Let me try to explain this by returning to the issue with which I concluded my construction of the dialectical dispute between Locke and Winstanley in that chapter.

Fig. 5: David Frazer, *Happy Hour* (2017)

7

Capital, Alienation, and the Nature of Our Political Ideals

THE ISSUE I RESTED with at the end of chapter 2 was prompted by the claim that rationality requires us to not pay the cost of co-operation needed for the collective cultivation of the commons and, therefore, it was rationality – and nothing less – that generated the tragedy of the commons. A standard response to this claim, I said, was that the commons need not be doomed to tragedy by this line of argument and that all it showed was that we require the law and its application in the policing and punishment of non-cooperation. Though I readily agreed to the necessity of such regulation – who wouldn't? – I also said that the Lockean tradition could point out that policing and punishment require co-operation, and if it is the refusal of co-operation that undermines the commons, then policing and punishment too would be susceptible to the same undermining, if the mentality was in play. As a result of this impasse, I suggested that perhaps a deeper exploration should be undertaken in which we inquire as to what is so compulsory about that mentality.

I then argued that the very idea of laws and norms and their implementation via policing and punishing in the social life of a group is something that occurs in a foreground of explicit discursive formulations that could not so much as be conceived and understood without a background of more implicit and by and large non-discursive practices of the group that I described as comprising a cultural commons. I further argued that these practices in the cultural commons are characterised by a pervasive relation of trust among individuals in the group, and it is this that underlies and makes possible the implementation of regulation via laws and norms, wherever such regulation occurs in the foreground. But I then stepped back to say that though "trust" is a useful and handy term to describe these relations of the cultural commons in the background (and "co-operation" the standard term to describe what is needed to keep the land and other commons from being undermined in the foreground), these terms, for one reason or another, don't get quite the right description of the underlying feature of the cultural commons that allows them to play their role in making regulation possible in the foreground.

Let's, then, go back to see how best to describe and understand the mentality that is central to the idea of rationality that the argument for the tragedy of the commons invokes, in order to undermine the idea of the commons and their collective cultivation. The crucial step I identified in the argument was when the commoner is supposed to have the driving anxiety and qualm: "What if I co-operated and others did not? That would be the worst possible outcome for me!" So, we should be asking: What does an anxiety and qualm of this sort reflect or reveal? And rather than simply say it reveals a lack of trust and a refusal to co-operate (saying that is hardly informative since we already know this from the general thrust of the argument's direction and conclusion), we should look for a deeper underlying malaise that prompts an anxiety of this kind.

There is a completely intuitive and familiar description of this malaise that is available from many of the writings of Marx and a wide legacy of Marxian thought influenced by his work, the *Economic and Philosophical Manuscripts of 1844*.[1] Though Marx in that work was focused on the conditions of labour in particular and was therefore speaking primarily of the affliction of a particular class, even just a slight abstraction from that specific context suggests the following wholly natural thought: it is only if individuals in a group were deeply *alienated* from each other that they would be prompted to anxiously ask, "What if I co-operated and others did not?'[2] This suggests that if the cultural commons were doing their work, and one were to get past the mentality that "rationality" requires of us in the argument of the tragedy of the commons, the ideal expressed in the cultural commons would be the ideal of an "*un*alienated mentality". And, conversely, there is no better elaboration of this mentality than to

[1] Karl Marx, *Economic and Philosophical Manuscripts of 1844* (from notes written in 1844, first published 1932; rpntd New York: Prometheus Publications, 1988).

[2] In fact, though Marx did focus primarily on the alienation of labour, he thought that alienation afflicted all classes, though obviously the symptoms of the malaise may well be quite distinct in different classes. I am fastening, however, on a symptom that generalises over all classes.

say that if one is unalienated, the question or qualm – What if I pay the cost of co-operation and others do not? – *would not so much as occur to one*. I emphasise these last few words deliberately. The idea, as I said, is not that it is morally wrong for that thought or question to occur to one. It is rather simply that the thought or question, if one is unalienated, *does not compute*.

I repeat, then, that the point is cognitive, not moral. To stress "unalienatedness" as a mentality is to stress something quite different from other ideals, like fraternity or solidarity with others, different from the demand that we shun self-interest and regard the interests of others. It is a more abstract ideal, one of a certain form of thinking and mentality within which anxieties of the sort that drive the argument that renders co-operation irrational are simply pre-empted from surfacing in one's own mind. Thus, one is not simply countering non-cooperation with the idea of co-operation. It is not a contest of opposing ideals in the foreground. One is claiming rather that non-cooperation emerges from an underlying malaise, a deformation of mentality that we call "alienation", and that the anxiety that leads "rationally" to non-cooperation is a symptom of that malaise, indeed that game theory, therefore, may itself be a higher-order symptom of the malaise. One is claiming, moreover, that the overcoming of the malaise and the attaining of the ideal of unalienatedness is a cognitive achievement, the achievement of a mentality or way of thinking, itself, no doubt, in turn, greatly facilitated by fundamental transformations in society. Marx himself famously argued that nothing less than the establishing of a classless society would make for the cognitive achievement that characterises the unalienated life. If fraternity and solidarity are relevant, it is in the forging of movements and a politics that bring these fundamental transformations in society, but they are not the ideals that are central to the analysis of the cultural commons and the ideal of unalienatedness that they exemplify. Fraternity and solidarity are, no doubt, good things, but not all good things are the same good thing, and being unalienated is a quite different kind of (good) thing. I'll say a little more about what sort of highly unusual good thing or ideal it is in a moment, but let me first say why the relevance of Marx to what I have just said above should now perhaps be obvious.

That there is no overcoming alienation until capitalism is in some sense transcended is immediately apparent when we raise a question that naturally arises out of the argument I have been developing: If the background has the resources I have been specifying to make possible the law and its implementation in the foreground (a possibility, as I said, that can appear to be threatened if our gaze is only on the foreground), why has it not and does it not have the same efficacy in making possible, in the foreground, the co-operation needed for the collective cultivation of the land commons or the environmental commons? The answer – with regard to the land commons – is precisely given by the entire range of changes that constitute the rise of capital in early modern Europe, which pre-empted their extensive collective cultivation, a pre-empting whose justification in a tradition of thought from Locke to Hardin we have been examining. And though the answer – with regard to the environmental commons – should acknowledge that the particular socialist experiments of the Soviet Union and the countries under its influence share the responsibility with corporate capital for the crisis of the environmental commons, the destruction of the environment is not endemic to the socialist ideal as such, whereas, as Marx pointed out in the *Grundrisse*,[3] it is endemic to the capitalist economic formation. The key difference, then, between what the presence of certain features in the cultural commons in the background has and has not made possible in the foreground is that what it has made possible (the law and its regulative implementation) is needed for the interests of capital itself, whereas the innate tendency of capital is to tolerate neither the extensive collective cultivation of the land commons nor the deep constrain-

[3] "For the first time, nature becomes purely an object for humankind, purely a matter of utility; ceases to be recognised as a power for itself; and the theoretical discovery of its autonomous laws appears merely as a ruse so as to subjugate it under human needs" is how he describes this aspect of capitalism as an economic formation. See Karl Marx, *Grundrisse* (written 1857–8; first published in Russian in 2 vols, 1939 and 1941; English translation 1973; rpntd New York: Vintage Press, 1974).

ing of its drive for private gain and profit that would be necessary for preserving the environmental commons.[4]

The chief focus and theme of this book on the commons, however, are not the transformations needed in a longstanding economic formation of modernity but the nature and location and role of the ideals that are sought in these transformations. And I am keen, therefore, that my own talk of how the ideal of unalienatedness consists in an overcoming of a malaise of mentality in the modern period[5] should not give any impression that the malaise is so comprehensive that there are no contexts in the quotidian practices and relations in the background where the malaise has never really formed in the mentalities of individuals in the group. Unalienatedness is a common feature of their habitual and unselfconscious relations with one another. It is in fact

[4] How deep? My own instinct, based on a reading of the most plausible and convincing of the literature on today's environmental concerns, is that they are likely to need to be so deep that they may amount to a terminus of capitalism not only as we know it today, but as we have known it for the centuries during which it has thrived.

[5] I say "in the modern period" but don't intend that to contrast with alienation in the pre-modern period. I follow most of the prominent thinkers who have written on alienation (Rousseau, Hegel, Marx, Sartre, etc.) in assuming that alienation is a malaise of the modern period. Whatever undoubtedly great and horrific oppression serfs and even slaves suffered in pre-modernity, a lack of belonging is not assumed to be one of them.

their natural way of being in many contexts of their everyday lives.

To elaborate a little more fully the ideal of unalienated life, which I am at pains to distinguish from other ideals – whether fraternity and solidarity or liberty and equality – permit me the indulgence of a personal anecdote, which I have written about elsewhere, to make a quite different point.[6] It concerns an experience with my father when I was a boy of around twelve. He would sometimes ask that I go for walks with him in the early morning on the beach near our home in Bombay. One day, while walking, we came across a wallet with some rupees sticking out of it. My father stopped me and said, somewhat dramatically, "Akeel, why shouldn't we take this?" And I said sheepishly, though honestly, "I think we should take it." He looked irritated and said, "Why do you think we should take it?" And I replied with what is surely a classic response, "Because if we don't take it, somebody else will." I expected a denunciation, but his irritation passed and he said: "If we don't take it, nobody else will." I thought then that this remark had no logic to it at all. Only decades later when I was thinking of questions of alienation

[6] In my essay "Gandhi, the Philosopher", in Akeel Bilgrami, *Secularism, Identity, and Enchantment* (Boston: Harvard University Press, and Ranikhet: Permanent Black, 2014), where I mention it in order to elaborate Gandhi's conception of ethics as moral exemplarity rather than as moral imperatives.

did I realise that his remark reflected an unalienated framework of thinking.

The "nobody else will" in my father's response cannot be expressive of unalienatedness if it is interpreted as a prediction of what others will do. When we predict what others will do, we relate to them from a disengaged perspective. That is the perspective that pervades alienated social relations. In fact, it is only when we view others from this perspective that we are prompted to ask the question that drives the tragedy of the commons: What if I pay the cost of co-operation and others don't? From a detached perspective, what my father said might seem like naïve optimism about what others will do. But the assumption that others will not take the wallet if we don't or that others will co-operate if we do is not made from that detached point of view. It is an assumption of a quite different sort, more in the spirit of "let's see ourselves this way", an assumption that is unselfconsciously expressive of our unalienatedness, of our being engaged with others and the world, rather than assessing, in a detached mode, the prospects of how they will behave. My father was suggesting, in other words, that my grounds for my response to his question is a reflection of just the kind of falling short of the ideal of unalienatedness that I am claiming is reflected in the question that is supposed to occur to the rational commoner in a certain conception of social and political rationality that drives the considerations that lead to the tragedy of the commons.

The striking thing about this is that when the ideal of unalienatedness, so understood, is working, it does not seem to even be an ideal. It is only when we fall away from it, as in my declared grounds for taking the wallet, or the commoner's driving anxiety about whether others will co-operate or not, that unalienatedness appears as an ideal, something my father needed *to say*. This is the point I have been harping on when I have consistently characterised the background of the cultural commons as being largely non-discursive and tacit. In this sense, the ideal of unalienatedness, which the cultural commons exemplify, is quite unlike even some of our most central ideals, such as liberty and equality, that find their constant and explicit articulations in codes and constitutions and "policies".

This point about the ideal not appearing to be an ideal when it is working becomes clear if we draw an analogy with a point that Wittgenstein makes in his well-known discussion of the notion of a "basic action" in the characterisation of human intentionality. Wittgenstein claimed that one could not understand intentionality as it applies to human actions unless one understood the idea of what he called a "basic action". A basic action is something you do, and you don't do anything else in virtue of which you do it. So, adapting a famous example of his,[7] let's take

[7] See Wittgenstein, *Philosophical Investigations* (1953; rpntd Oxford: Wiley-Blackwell, 2009), 1, 621.

my intentional action of waving to a friend. Wittgenstein says philosophers have tended to say that an intentional action like waving to a friend conceptually breaks down to more basic actions such as, say, my moving my arm, and then even more basic (non-action) events such as my arm moving. On their view, the philosophical picture is that *the arm going up* is basic and to it successive intentions accrue. The first intention to accrue might be: I intend that my arm move. That yields the non-basic action of my moving my arm. The next accretion to this is the intention that – *by moving my arm* – I wave to a friend. That, in turn, yields the even less basic action of *my waving to a friend.* And Wittgenstein says that this picture of intentional action is all wrong. He says if I wave to a friend, the basic action *just is the waving to a friend.* That's it. There is no other action in virtue of which I do it. So, in the standard cases of intentional action, there is no breaking down of intentional action into more and more basic action components.

Now, someone might object: Why are you wheeling in this analogy with Wittgenstein? It is completely irrelevant. Your subject is *normative*, an ideal, the ideal of an unalienated mentality, which you say is exemplified in the relations and practices that comprise the cultural commons. Wittgenstein is not talking of an ideal at all. He is talking of the nature of intentional action, which he says is a "basic" action that can't conceptually be broken down into more basic actions. But this objection misses the point

Fig. 6: David Frazer, *Wounded Wood II* (2017)

both of what Wittgenstein is saying and what I take the ideal of an unalienated mentality to be. Wittgenstein is indeed talking of something normative as well, an ideal. It's just that it does not look like an ideal when it is working. And we can bring this out by imagining a case when the ideal is not working. Suppose that I have been recently estranged from my friend. And suppose I want to recover normal friendly relations again. Well, given the estrangement, there is a kind of shrinkage in me, and I may not be able to just wave to him with the same unselfconscious, easy, act that I usually do when I see him across the quad. Hence, I may think: let me move my arm in a vigorous way and hope that it comes off as a friendly waving. In such cases, I have lapsed from the ideal because of the estrangement and the ensuing shrinkage in me, and the moving of the arm rather than the waving to a friend is indeed the basic action. It is a case of having lapsed from the ideal of intentionality in action that Wittgenstein has proposed. It's just that in the normal cases, when there is no shrinkage, everything proceeds in the waving unselfconsciously and easily, and we do not even notice that an ideal is being exemplified. Only the lapses from the ideal bring out that an ideal is at stake and in play in what Wittgenstein has proposed. The situation is exactly the same with unalienatedness. When the ideal is working it does not seem to be an ideal, and the qualm (What if I co-operated and others did not?) does not occur to individuals in the group. But if the qualm does occur to us, we are suddenly alerted to having run up against an ideal from which we have lapsed.

It is precisely because of this exceptional feature of the ideal of an unalienated life and mentality that one cannot insert the ideal into a constitution (as has been done with a wide range of other ideals, such as free speech) or even into a slogan (as has been done with liberty, equality, fraternity). One cannot even do with it what Tutu and Mandela sought to do with trust in their remarkable model for transitional justice as non-forensic engagement with perpetrators of crime in which trust was explicitly inserted into the formulation of the point of its confessional procedure. The unalienated lives and mentality are essentially non-discursive ways of being that characterise our practices in the background. When they go missing and we are suddenly reminded, as a result, that they do amount to an ideal, we of course speak explicitly of alienation and the ideal of overcoming it, and write lengthy academic papers about it, but when they work as an ideal, they are unspoken. As Marx says in his writings on the subject, being unalienated is an ideal that is constitutive of what we are when we are most representatively human. It is not an optional ideal, it is not a cancellable ideal; to deny it is to deny our species being. When we lapse from it (often extensively, as we have), we may need to strive to transform the institutions and social and economic formations that have induced the alienation. Marx himself had a detailed and rightly famous

Fig. 7: David Frazer, *Looking Out at the Rain, Another Hour Gone* (2017)

diagnosis, as we know, of what does induce it and what has to be transformed. Those are the large and urgent issues that beset us in our modernity and set us our practical tasks. All I have sought to do is to see through the *conceptual* implications for the ideal itself when we see the lapse from the ideal as manifest in one of the most frequently expressed (and theoretically mobilised) anxieties in the foreground of our social lives in modernity: What if I co-operate and others do not?

Fig. 8: David Frazer, *Adrift* (2016)

Coda

IF I AM RIGHT that we are, in many contexts of our quotidian background practices, thoroughly unalienated in our mentality, that implies that this anxiety – What if I paid the cost of co-operation and others did not?" – does not occur to us in many contexts of our everyday lives. These are the contexts that comprise what I have called the "cultural commons".

This implies, in turn, that we go in and out of being alienated. In some contexts we are unalienated, in others we are not. Part of the problem with the periodisation of social histories in large "stages" or slabs of categorised time is that modernity comes to be presented as having a comprehensive reach and, as a result, talk of alienation is made to seem (for instance, by Horkheimer and Adorno[1]) as if it has penetrated all the ground there is in the modern period. I have tried, in this book, to present a way of resisting that theoretical understanding of the issues at stake. A useful alternative theoretical understanding might be to invoke a notion that psychologists call a "frame", which will allow us to acknowledge the pockets of unalienatedness even in the midst of our alienated modernity that we so lament.

[1] See my earlier reference to Foucault in chapter 6, which was roughly on the same point, of viewing a whole era as passing over into another, though I was not there talking of alienation. Such a view seems to go hand in hand with the idea that an era, properly described as "modernity", would find these effects emerging in the new "episteme" as comprehensive.

A "frame" is an insulated space within which thoughts occur, sealed off from other such spaces in the thinking of the same individual subject. As a result, the individual may have quite inconsistent thoughts but, being in different frames, they are not acknowledged or felt to be inconsistent by the individual. From the first-person point of view, consistency and inconsistency occur only within frames, not across frames, so the subject does not assess for consistency and inconsistency straddling the frames. Thus, just to give an example, someone might perceive poverty and homelessness as they drive through Harlem and express the most humane and compassionate desire to uplift the people into better conditions of living. Yet, if asked whether there should be public expenditure to uplift Harlem's poor residents, he might recoil from the thought with horror. In one frame, the quotidian one, he expresses great humanity; in the other – no doubt shaped by some course he has taken in economics or by what he has read in the prevalent media – he expresses the orthodoxies in the public air. He has no idea he is being inconsistent because the two thoughts are in different, insulated frames.[2]

[2] In seeing this as a framing issue, I am assuming, for the sake of argument – and surely the assumption is right in many actual cases of people making such responses – that such a person's refusal of public expenditure is not accompanied by his possession of any detailed opinions or theory about how upliftment of people in such conditions can actually be brought about by policies other than a commitment to public expenditure. Of course, one may

I am suggesting, similarly, that in one frame of thinking the thought "What if I co-operate and others do not?" may not occur to someone, but the same person might have just that anxiety while deliberating in another frame.

What this suggests is that, quite apart from the goals that a politics might have in seeking a material transformation of society to remove the underlying material causes of alienation of the modern period, when the goal of politics is also to address the consciousness of human subjects (which it surely must also be so that human subjectivity is moved to undertake those transformative struggles), then a humane politics should equally be seeking to remove the boundaries between these frames that seal them off from one another, so that an individual consciousness thinks in a unified frame and thereby comes to perceive its own inconsistencies. It is only this that will allow for the further deliberation by which individuals might be able to bring to bear the resources of their mentality in what was one frame (the one

---

doubt (as I do) that there are any plausible alternative policies to public expenditure in the context of the societies and economies we actually live in, but that is not the point. The point is only that there are many who do express these refusals of public expenditure while also displaying humane commitments to upliftment, each in a different frame, and if they were to be alerted to their inconsistency in doing so, they would indeed accept that they were being inconsistent without knowing it, rather than claim that they all along had a different view of how the upliftment might be brought about.

I have tended to attribute to the cultural commons in the background and its practices) to critical use in shaping the mentality in what used to be the other frame (what I have called the more foregrounded field where public policy is explicitly shaped and formulated).

Fig. 9: David Frazer, *Passing Storm* (2016)

ASHOKA UNIVERSITY

HEDGEHOG AND FOX

HISTORY AND POLITICS SERIES

"The fox knows many things,
but the hedgehog knows one big thing"

General Editor

RUDRANGSHU MUKHERJEE

MONOGRAPHS

Steven I. Wilkinson ARMY AND NATION
Thomas R. Trautmann ELEPHANTS AND KINGS
Partha Chatterjee, Sudipta Kaviraj, Nivedita Menon
THE INDIAN IDEOLOGY
Nayanjot Lahiri ASHOKA IN ANCIENT INDIA
Nicholas B. Dirks AUTOBIOGRAPHY OF AN ARCHIVE
Vasudha Dalmia HINDU PASTS
Dipesh Chakrabarty THE CALLING OF HISTORY
Sunil Agnani HATING EMPIRE PROPERLY
Mahesh Rangarajan NATURE AND NATION
Bhavani Raman DOCUMENT RAJ
Sumit Guha BEYOND CASTE
Iqtidar Alam Khan INDIA'S POLITY IN THE AGE OF AKBAR
Linda Hess BODIES OF SONG

Charu Gupta THE GENDER OF CASTE

Ajay Skaria UNCONDITIONAL EQUALITY

Velcheru Narayana Rao TEXT AND TRADITION IN SOUTH INDIA

Udaya Kumar WRITING THE FIRST PERSON

Chinya V. Ravishankar SONS OF SARASVATI

Christian Lee Novetzke THE QUOTIDIAN REVOLUTION

B.D. Chattopadhyaya THE CONCEPT OF BHARATVARSHA

Sumit Sarkar ESSAYS OF A LIFETIME

Sudhir Mahadevan A VERY OLD MACHINE

Sanjay Subrahmanyam EMPIRES BETWEEN ISLAM AND CHRISTIANITY

Neeladri Bhattacharya THE GREAT AGRARIAN CONQUEST

Chetan Singh HIMALAYAN HISTORIES

Yogendra Yadav MAKING SENSE OF INDIAN DEMOCRACY

Arvind Krishna Mehrotra TRANSLATING THE INDIAN PAST

Francis Robinson THE MUSLIM WORLD IN MODERN SOUTH ASIA

Joya Chatterji PARTITION'S LEGACIES

Jennifer Dubrow COSMOPOLITAN DREAMS

Sumit Guha HISTORY AND COLLECTIVE MEMORY IN SOUH ASIA 1200–2000

Partha Chatterjee I AM THE PEOPLE

Mohammed Ayoob and Danielle N. Lussier THE MANY FACES OF POLITICAL ISLAM

Sherali Tareen DEFENDING MUHAMMAD IN MODERNITY

Shekhar Pathak THE CHIPKO MOVEMENT

Muzaffar Alam THE SUFIS AND THE MUGHALS

Partha Chatterjee THE TRUTHS AND LIES OF NATIONALISM

G. Kanato Chophy CHRISTIANITY AND POLITICS IN TRIBAL INDIA

Harjot Oberoi WHEN DOES HISTORY BEGIN?
Niraja Gopal Jayal CITIZENSHIP IMPERILLED
Tanika Sarkar HINDU NATIONALISM IN INDIA
Sudipta Kaviraj THE POLITICS OF GOD (forthcoming)
Angela Xavier RELIGION AND EMPIRE IN PORTUGUESE INDIA
Vinayak Chaturvedi HINDUTVA AND VIOLENCE
Corinne Lefèvre CONSOLIDATING EMPIRE
Xinru Liu EARLY BUDDHIST SOCIETY
Nayanjot Lahiri TRAVELLING WITH ASHOKA (forthcoming)
A.R. Venkatachalapathy THE SHORT HISTORY OF A VERY BIG BOOK (forthcoming)
Rahul Markovits A PASSAGE TO EUROPE (forthcoming)
Swati Ganguly TAGORE'S UNIVERSITY
Pulapre Balakrishnan INDIA'S ECONOMY FROM NEHRU TO MODI
Akeel Bilgrami CAPITAL, CULTURE, AND THE COMMONS (forthcoming)
Syed Sayeed REFLECTIONS ON AMBEDKAR'S "ANNIHILATION OF CASTE"

INDIAN HISTORY and POLITICS CLASSICS

Ranajit Guha A RULE OF PROPERTY FOR BENGAL
Ranajit Guha THE SMALL VOICE OF HISTORY
Romila Thapar THE PAST BEFORE US
Muzaffar Alam THE LANGUAGES OF POLITICAL ISLAM IN INDIA
Asok Sen ISWAR CHANDRA VIDYASAGAR AND HIS ELUSIVE MILESTONES
Rosalind O'Hanlon CASTE CONFLICT AND IDEOLOGY
Arvind K. Mehrotra, ed. A CONCISE HISTORY OF INDIAN LITERATURE IN ENGLISH
Ramachandra Guha AN ANTHROPOLOGIST AMONG THE MARXISTS

Partha Chatterjee DEAD MAN WANDERING

Partha Chatterjee EMPIRE AND NATION

Partha Chatterjee THE BLACK HOLE OF EMPIRE

M.S.S. Pandian BRAHMIN AND NON-BRAHMIN

Nayanjot Lahiri FINDING FORGOTTEN CITIES

Iqtidar Alam Khan THE MUGHAL NOBILITY

Srinath Raghavan WAR AND PEACE IN MODERN INDIA

Sudipta Kaviraj THE ENCHANTMENT OF DEMOCRACY AND INDIA

Sudipta Kaviraj THE IMAGINARY INSTITUTION OF INDIA

Sudipta Kaviraj TRAJECTORIES OF THE INDIAN STATE

Sudipta Kaviraj THE INVENTION OF PRIVATE LIFE

David Hardiman GANDHI IN HIS TIME AND OURS

Christophe Jaffrelot INDIA'S SILENT REVOLUTION

Sunil Kumar THE EMERGENCE OF THE DELHI SULTANATE

Christian Lee Novetzke HISTORY, BHAKTI, AND PUBLIC MEMORY

Ramchandra Gandhi THE AVAILABILITY OF RELIGIOUS IDEAS

Brijen Kumar Gupta SIRAJ-UD-DAULAH AND THE EAST INDIA COMPANY

Francis Robinson THE ULAMA OF FARANGI MAHALL AND ISLAM IN SOUTH ASIA

Niraja Gopal Jayal CITIZENSHIP AND ITS DISCONTENTS

Michael J. Fisher COUNTERFLOWS TO COLONIALISM

Jahnavi Phalkey ATOMIC STATE

Ramachandra Guha THE UNQUIET WOODS

Rudrangshu Mukherjee AWADH IN REVOLT

Sarvepalli Gopal IMPERIALISTS, NATIONALISTS, DEMOCRATS

Sheldon Pollock THE LANGUAGE OF THE GODS IN THE WORLD OF MEN

HISTORICAL SOURCEBOOKS IN CLASSICAL INDIAN THOUGHT

Patrick Olivelle, ed. A DHARMA READER

Sheldon Pollock, ed. A RASA READER

Johannes Bronkhorst, ed. A SABDA READER

INTERNATIONAL CLASSICS

Joan Sales UNCERTAIN GLORY
Jaan Kross THE CZAR'S MADMAN
Arvind K. Mehrotra, ed. THE BOOK OF INDIAN ESSAYS
Sálim Ali WORDS FOR BIRDS, ed. Tara Gandhi